I CAN BE A WRITER

I Can Be a Copywriter

Meeg Pincus

Published in the United States of America by:

CHERRY LAKE PRESS
2395 South Huron Parkway, Suite 200, Ann Arbor, Michigan 48104
www.cherrylakepress.com

Reading Adviser: Beth Walker Gambro, MS, Ed., Reading Consultant, Yorkville, IL

Photo Credits: © 5 PenguinLens/Shutterstock; © Bodleian Libraries, University of Oxford via CC BY-NC 4.0, 6; © Artography/Shutterstock, 7; © Sorbis/Shutterstock, 8 (left); © JJava Designs/Shutterstock, 8 (right); © Pressmaster/Dreamstime.com, 9; © YAKOBCHUK VIACHESLAV/Shutterstock, 11; © Urbanscape/Shutterstock, 12; © Friends Stock/Shutterstock, 13; © BalazsSebok/Shutterstock, 14; © CarlosBarquero/Shutterstock, 15; © Paul Mckinnon/Dreamstime.com, 16; © fast-stock/Shutterstock, 18; © Daisy Daisy/Shutterstock, 20; Wikimedia Commons, Public Domain, 21; © Roman Motizov/Shutterstock, 22

Copyright © 2026 by Cherry Lake Publishing Group

All rights reserved. No part of this book may be reproduced or utilized in any form or by any means without written permission from the publisher.

Cherry Lake Press is an imprint of Cherry Lake Publishing Group.

Library of Congress Cataloging-in-Publication Data has been filed and is available at catalog.loc.gov

Cherry Lake Publishing Group would like to acknowledge the work of the Partnership for 21st Century Learning, a Network of Battelle for Kids. Please visit Battelle for Kids online for more information.

Printed in the United States of America

Note from publisher: Websites change regularly, and their future contents are outside of our control. Supervise children when conducting any recommended online searches for extended learning opportunities.

CONTENTS

What Do Copywriters Do?	4
Why Would I Want to Write Copy?	10
How Can I Learn to Write Copy?	17
Activity	22
Find Out More	23
About the Author	23
Glossary	24
Index	24

WHAT DO COPYWRITERS DO?

Have you ever gotten excited about a game, food, or **cause** from an advertisement, or ad, you saw? Can you repeat a famous line about a certain **brand**? Do you love a clever TV commercial?

Then you have seen what copywriters do!

Copy is the text used to sell something. Whether it's a billboard, magazine ad, or a commercial, a copywriter wrote the words behind it.

What would you write an ad for?

Copywriting is as old as the printing press. The very first known printed advertisement is from 1476. It sold a booklet for priests in England. The ad was made to be hung on walls and doors.

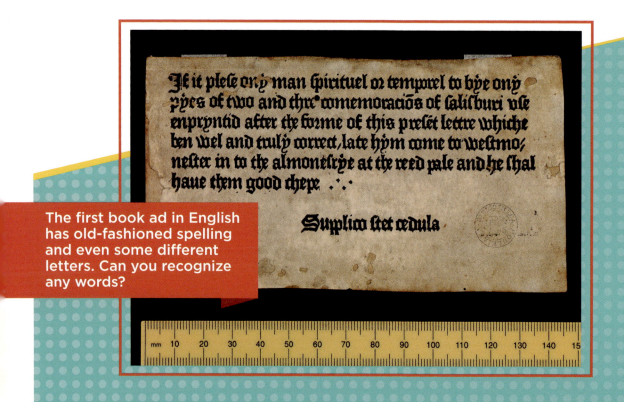

The first book ad in English has old-fashioned spelling and even some different letters. Can you recognize any words?

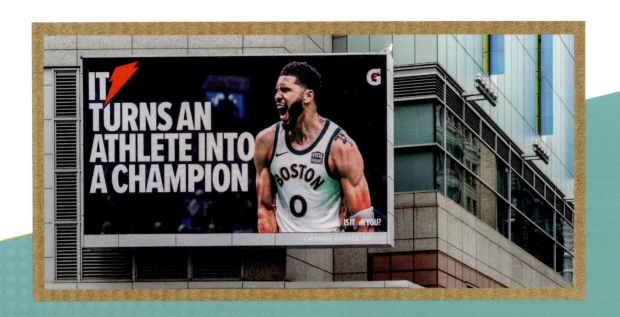

Copywriters write to **persuade**. They use words to inspire people to buy a product or service, or to take a specific action. Actions today could be to visit a store or website, sign up for texts, or donate to a cause.

Make a Guess!

Why do you think copywriting has been around for so long? Who benefits from copywriting?

Copywriters write copy that is clear and taps into people's feelings.

Copy can be as short as a **tagline**, also called a slogan or catchphrase. Think "Just Do It" for Nike, or "i'm lovin' it" for McDonald's.

Other copy can be as long as a full **brochure** or website. It can tell people's stories of how a product helped them or describe an organization's history and **values**.

Think!

Do you feel that it's healthy for kids to have product ads and taglines targeted at them? Why or why not?

Brochures explain a product or event in detail.

WHY WOULD I WANT TO WRITE COPY?

Do you like to write short pieces rather than long ones? Is it fun for you to think up catchy or funny taglines? Are you curious about people and why they do things? Do you enjoy the creative challenge of persuading others?

Then you may want to write copy!

Copywriters help companies connect with their customers.

Being a copywriter means working with many other people. If you work well with others, you may enjoy this writing field.

Copywriters work with other writers and artists to **brainstorm** creative ideas for ads and **campaigns**. They also work with different **clients** who hire them.

Do you like variety and learning about new things? As a copywriter, you must quickly learn about different projects and think of fresh ideas.

You also have to be curious about people and listen to them. To persuade someone, you must understand their problems, needs, and what motivates them to try something new.

Ask Questions!

Show an ad to a family member or friend. Ask them what the ad says to them. Ask if and how it persuades them to do something.

Different people have different problems, needs, and motivations. How might that affect ads targeting them?

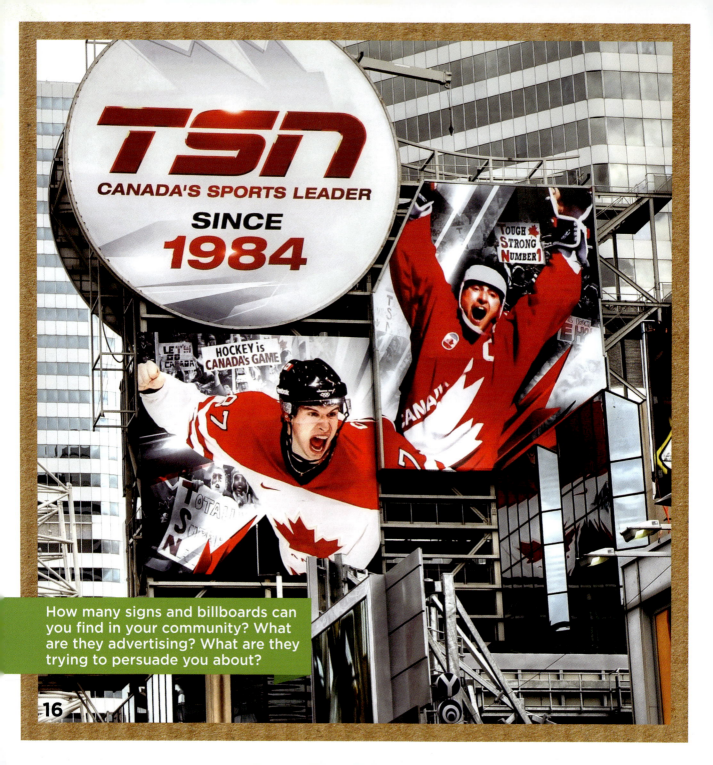

How many signs and billboards can you find in your community? What are they advertising? What are they trying to persuade you about?

HOW CAN I LEARN TO WRITE COPY?

Copy is everywhere! Start to really pay attention to ads, commercials, and any copy trying to persuade you to buy or do something.

Ask yourself: Do they use humor? Do they tap into a problem or issue that people have? Is there a catchy line that sticks in your memory?

Write and share with friends. Test out new ideas.

Becoming a copywriter means being both a good writer and a student of human behavior.

The more you write, the better writer you will become. Any kind of writing helps! Write stories or cartoons, speeches or jokes—just write often.

Also, pay attention to the people around you. Think about why they do things and what they really need and want. Try to identify the emotions people have and write to those feelings.

Look!

Look at a magazine's ads. What do the images tell you? How do they work with the copy to persuade readers?

Improv and drama classes let you practice being creative.

20

You can take classes in all kinds of writing. Classes in speech and debate can also help sharpen your persuasive skills. And **improv** classes can help you learn to think fast, listen, and respond to others!

Can you be a copywriter? If you want to learn to write creative, catchy text that helps persuade people... yes, you can!

Think different.

ACTIVITY

Choose something you'd like to persuade others to like as much as you do. It can be a food, a game, a book, an important cause—anything that sparks your creativity!

Then write copy for a campaign to persuade others to buy your product or take an action. Your campaign will consist of three parts:

1) A tagline or catchphrase (1 phrase)

2) An ad for a magazine (3 to 5 short sentences—with drawings, if you like!)

3) A radio or TV commercial (a 30-second script—read it aloud to time it!)

Think about why people need or want this thing and what feelings they might have about it. Try using humor or a story. Get creative and have fun!

FIND OUT MORE

Books

Barton, Bethany. *Give Bees a Chance.* New York, NY: Viking, 2017.

Bouler, Olivia. *Olivia's Birds: Saving the Gulf.* New York, NY: Sterling Children's Books, 2011.

Furlong, Sarah, and David Rhodes. *A Kids Book About Advertising.* Portland, OR: A Kid's Co. Books, 2023.

Websites

With an adult, explore more online with these suggested searches.

"Best Ads Directed Toward Children" videos, *Ad Forum*

Free travel brochure activity and template, *Layers of Learning*

ABOUT THE AUTHOR

Meeg Pincus loves to write. She is the author of more than 30 books for children. She has been a writer and editor for books, newspapers, magazines, and more. She also loves to sing, make art, and hang out with her family, friends, and adorable dog.

GLOSSARY

brainstorm (BRAYN-stohrm) activity of coming up with and sharing ideas

brand (BRAND) unique identity for a business, organization, or individual

brochure (broh-SHUHR) small booklet used to advertise a product or service

campaigns (kam-PAYNS) series of planned activities to achieve a goal

cause (KAHZ) social issue or problem that people actively work to improve

clients (KLYE-uhnts) people or companies who pay for one's services

improv (IM-prahv) a type of comedy that is unscripted and requires quick thinking and teamwork; short for improvisation

persuade (per-SWAYD) to convince someone of an idea or course of action through argument or request

tagline (TAG-lieyn) short, memorable phrase identified with a product or brand

values (VAL-yooz) ideas and beliefs that are most important to a person or group

INDEX

activities, 22
advertising, 4–9, 12, 14–15, 16, 17, 21, 22

billboards, 4, 7, 14, 16
brochures, 6, 9

classes, 20–21
commercials, 4, 17, 22

copywriters, 4–9, 12–14, 19, 21, 22
copywriting, 4, 6, 7, 10, 12
creativity, 10, 12, 14, 20–21, 22

human behavior and needs, 7–8, 10, 14–15, 17, 19, 22

learning, 17–21

magazine ads, 4, 19, 22

persuasion, 7–8, 10, 14, 16, 17, 21, 22
print ads, 4, 6, 9, 19, 22

slogans, 4, 8, 10, 21, 22

taglines, 4, 8, 10, 21, 22
teamwork, 12–13

writing copy, 4–9, 10, 12, 14, 17–19, 21, 22